SPEEDY PHOEBE

A Carson Elementary Story

Illustrations and design by Matt Tooth
Edited by Geoff Byrd

Published by TWU Publishing
www.twupublishing.com

ISBN 979-8-89109-570-0 (paperback)
ISBN 979-8-89109-744-5 (hardcover)
ISBN 979-8-89109-571-7 (ebook)

Dedicated to all the kids, small and
large, with big dreams;
don't let anyone stand in your way,
not even yourself.

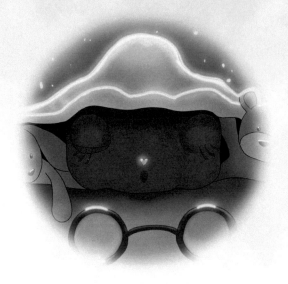

SPEEDY PHOEBE

Written by

Ryanne Siddiq

Illustrated by

Matt Tooth

Phoebe speeds around her house,
practicing for field day at Carson Elementary School.
She might be the smallest carlette, but she loves to go fast.
Phoebe can't WAIT for tomorrow's races!

"Easy there, speedster!"
Her dad waves a checkered flag.
"Great job practicing.
Let's get you to bed so you're rested for tomorrow."

Phoebe goes to sleep and dreams of being a great race car,

just like her dad.

After a good night's rest, Phoebe gets ready for school.
She drinks a healthy breakfast...

...gets extra clean (especially behind the wheels)...

...and even puts on her best racing tires!

On the drive to school,
Phoebe pops up and down like a lowrider.
She's so excited!

Her dad laughs and gives her
a big nudge when he drops her off.
"Ok my bouncy little racer.
Just do your best, and have tons of fun!"

She's all smiles as she rolls up to her class...
until she overhears her fellow carlettes.

"No carlette can match my power,
and everyone knows it!"
Roars Leo, spitting flames from his exhaust.

"You might be powerful Leo,
but I'm graceful like a ballerina!"
McKayla spins a few doughnuts.

Phoebe's smile falls.
She's not powerful like Leo,
nor as graceful as McKayla.
She's getting worried now.

Coach whistles to signal the first event is about to start.
Everyone heads over to the straight track for the drag race.

Phoebe lines up next to the others, a little nervous.

The whistle blows, and the racers take off.
Phoebe's tires spin and spin,
so she loses time and can't catch up!
She comes in
LAST
PLACE.

Her fellow carlettes laugh.

"Phoebe isn't strong enough to win a drag race." Leo snickers.

Phoebe feels embarrassed.

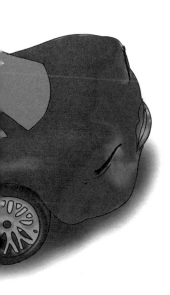

Coach whistles to signal the second event.
Everyone heads over to the circuit track for the agility race.

Phoebe sucks air into her engine
to get more power this time!

The whistle blows, and the racers take off.
She doesn't spin her wheels at the start,
but she isn't focused and takes the corners wrong.

LAST

PLACE

AGAIN.

"I can run circles around the rest of the carlettes."
McKayla sneers.

Phoebe is disappointed in herself.

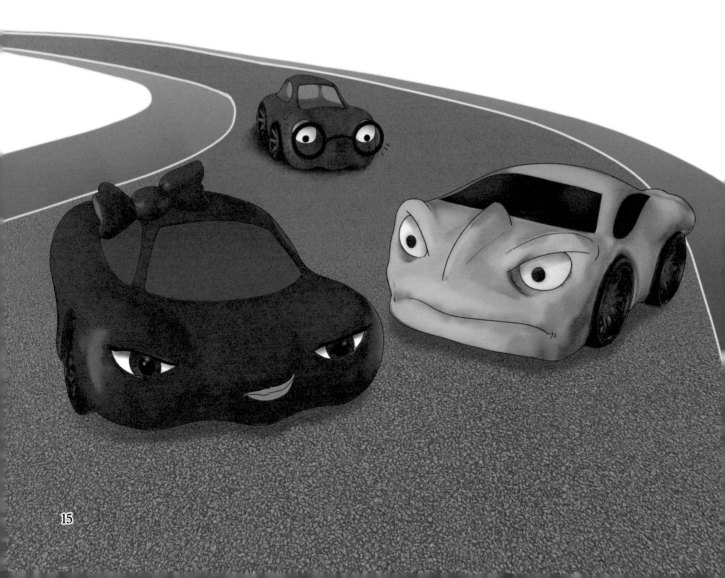

Coach blows the whistle for the last event.
Everyone heads over to the combo track for the endurance race.
This is usually Phoebe's favorite!

But Phoebe's engine sputters,
concerned her fellow carlettes are right about her.

She lines up next to the other carlettes anyway,
more determined than ever.

"I'm not the strongest, but I can shift gears really fast.
I'm little, but that makes me great around corners.
Besides, Dad said to do my best and have fun!
I can do that, even if I don't win the race."

Just as Phoebe starts to feel better, McKayla huffs,
"Why do you even bother to race, Phoebe?
You'll just come in last!"

"No. Not this time," she thinks to herself.
"I'm going to stop worrying about
what other cars think and just be myself.
I'm talented in my own way,
and I race with my heart, not just my wheels!"

The race starts, and Phoebe's renewed confidence helps her get a great start off the line! Leo loudly growls into the lead, but his noisy exhaust scares a mouse across the track.

"Leo! Look out!" Phoebe yells.

She can only watch as the tiny mouse terrifies not-so-brave Leo into a spin and off the track.

Phoebe continues racing close behind McKayla,
off the straight into the corners.
On the last corner, there is mud on the track
from where Leo spun out.

McKayla doesn't see it, and ends up covered in grime!

"EWW! Now I'm all dirty! I can't race looking like this!"
McKayla whines as she peels off the track.

Phoebe carefully steers around the mud and
crosses the finish line.

Then she asks the janitor to help Leo get unstuck.

And tells the nurse to check on McKayla who's all muddy.

Phoebe sighs in relief. She heads over to the podium knowing
her fellow carlettes are being helped.
She's surprised to hear the coach calling her name!

"You won the final race Phoebe!" Coach beams.

"I did?" Phoebe asks.

"That's not all Phoebe. You also win the
"Most Valuable Carlette" trophy.
You may have started slow, but you never gave up.
Congratulations Phoebe, you deserve it!"

Phoebe lights up in shock. "Really? Thanks Coach!"

"Congratulations on your win, Phoebe.
We underestimated you."
Patched-up Leo grumbles.

"Thanks for sending help, sorry we were so mean."
A freshly-cleaned McKayla mutters.

Phoebe grins. "Thanks for bringing out the best in me!"

The carlettes sheepishly smile back.

What a great day!
Phoebe let go of all her doubts, regained her courage,
and was able to become the MVC:
Most Valuable Carlette!

She also won over some new friends.

Phoebe's dreams of becoming a great race car are
a little bit closer, and her journey is just beginning.

PHOEBE

Age	7
Classification	Carlette
Speed	Speedy!
Favorite Race	One with corners
Top Trait	Never gives up
Favorite Food	Chocolate cake

LEO

Age	7
Classification	Carlette
Speed	Fast off the line
Favorite Race	Drag Race
Top Trait	Bold
Favorite Food	Pizza (duh!)

COACH

Age	Don't ask!
Classification	Minivan
Speed	Slow but steady
Favorite Race	Cross Country
Top Trait	Firm but fair
Favorite Food	Protein shakes

JANITOR

Age	Old but wise!
Classification	Garbage Truck
Speed	Clunky
Favorite Race	Eating competitions
Top Trait	Conventional wisdom
Favorite Food	Leftover spaghetti

McKAYLA

Age	7
Classification	Carlette
Speed	Quick and accurate
Favorite Race	Circuit Race
Top Trait	Graceful
Favorite Food	Macaroons

DAD

Age	41
Classification	Race Car
Speed	Stealthy
Favorite Race	Road Course
Top Trait	Confidence
Favorite Food	Steak (medium-rare)

NURSE

Age	38
Classification	Ambulance
Speed	Faster than you think!
Favorite Race	Time Attack
Top Trait	Compassion
Favorite Food	Granola bars

TEACHER

Age	57
Classification	Vintage Truck
Speed	Just cruisin'
Favorite Race	Chess Tournaments
Top Trait	Patience
Favorite Food	Coffee

Glossary

Carlette - A young car classmate

Circuit Race - A racetrack with both straightaways and curves

Drag Race - A straight racetrack that tests speed over a certain distance

Endurance Race - A longer race that includes more than one race type

Lowrider - A cool car with hydraulics that raises, lowers, and hops up and down!

Road Course - A race on closed streets instead of a racetrack

Spinning Donuts - A car spinning around in a tight circle

Spitting Flames - High powered cars with flames blasting from their exhaust

Time Attack - A race against the clock where the car with the fastest lap wins

JOEY

Age	7
Classification	Carlette
Speed	4-wheelin'!
Favorite Race	Off Road
Top Trait	Rugged
Favorite Food	Fried Chicken

Calling all Carlettes!

Want a free gift, to contact the author, or to learn more about the Carson Elementary world? Scan the QR code for all of this and more!

Made in the USA
Columbia, SC
26 January 2024

30971521R00020